LAMBRETTA LADIES'

MEMORIES OF LONG AGO

By the same Author
Taking in the View – Life from a Scooter

Lambretta Ladies – Memories of Long Ago
Copyright © Mark Bennett 2025
Round the Bend Publications

www.lifefromascooter.com

ISBN 978-1-0369-1341-0

Serendipity/noun:

The occurrence and development of events by chance,
in a happy or beneficial way.

At the drop of a hat, the tip of a wink
At the turning of the card
Serendipity told me, she'd be there

Serendipity – John Martyn

For Brenda and Arlene.
Original Scootergirls.

Photographs

1

WHERE TO START?

Music and scooters have been the two constants in my life since I discovered them both as a young teenager growing up in Cambridge. I found myself mixing in these two parallel and vibrant local scenes and they connected to give me direction in my increasingly independent, if sometimes wayward, youth. Riding my scooter around the city I would connect with other scooterists, establish friendships, and find myself travelling far and wide around the UK with them during those formative years. Where music was concerned, friendships were created through mates, in pubs where a matching band T-shirt would provide a connection with a fellow fan, or at one of the many music venues scattered around the area. At a gig I might end up in conversation with somebody I recognised from a previous event, or maybe while waiting to get served at the bar a chat would begin and sow the seeds of a new friendship. My social circle built over time, and in the days before the instant contact provided by mobile phones, I would visit local pubs on a Friday or Saturday night looking for my friends to share a drink or two with. If there were no scooter mates in The Kings Arms, I could cross the road to the Cambridge Arms or wander along to The Mitre looking for some psychobilly mates, who could normally be found sitting in their usual spot at the back of the pub.

Without scooters and without music, this book and the history of the two people within it would only be known to close family and friends from long ago. To lose their stories and the photographs of their time riding Lambrettas in the formative years of the scooter scene would be heart-rending. The tales of their travels on their scooters, along many of the roads that I would also enjoy, are included here. To lose the history of these people, their stories and the experiences that defined them, would be a great loss in our ever-changing world and to the story of such an iconic form of transport, that gave so much to so many people in the decades that would follow.

What brought this story to me was serendipity, and a series of fortunate events. Events that were spread over a timespan of nearly forty years. Events that I could never have connected together, until they themselves rounded the circle of time.

Way back in 1987 a friend, Andy Lindsay who like me enjoyed both scooters and music, told me about a friend of his whose band had just recorded and released a new single. With Andy's recommendation and the band being local my interest was sparked. All we had to do was walk to the bedsit of the friend and hand over a couple of quid for a copy of the record. The bedsit was on Mawson Road, just off Mill Road in Cambridge a culturally diverse and colourful part of the city, and the band was called the Fire Dept. The 7" disc of black plastic contained three songs; *GIRLGIRLGIRL!, GIRL AND A HOT-ROD!* and *WITCH-GIRL!* The band had a bit of a thing about girls, I think. There was a definite retro feel to the band, with the hot-rod, some sharp surf style guitar and the thumping Bo Diddleyish rhythm guitar within the title track. This trio of tunes was, and has been ever since, right up my street. The record label was a monotone collage of women's faces, the girls of the songs maybe, and I was given the promise of a picture sleeve when they were printed. I never received that sleeve and years later I would occasionally search the internet looking for another copy of that single with the elusive black and white picture sleeve.

The songs were energetic, always enjoyable to listen to, and would occasionally find their way onto various DIY compilation tapes that I put together over the years. But that record sleeve was always elusive. Over three decades later, while chatting to a newly arrived neighbour about music and record collection similarities, the Fire Dept. were mentioned by the guitar playing Gary O'Connor. He told me that he had spent some time in a band with one of their guitarists, Robin Taylor. Gary wore a look of amazement that I knew of the Fire Dept. and, when I produced the single that I had bought 35 years earlier, a promise was made to mention the missing sleeve to Robin when next seen.

Not long after that, while I was enjoying a beer with Gary at his home, I admired a sign written plaque adorning the wall of his kitchen and explained that I was looking for someone to paint a logo onto the side panels of a newly brought Lambretta. The scooter was built in Spain in 1956 and had been given the moniker of Minty by my wife Kerry, because of its colour. Robin's name was mentioned once again as being the person responsible for the sign written plaque, and I was given a phone number to make contact with him. Not long after, Minty was duly decorated with the words *Minty the Imperial* and *Fresco y Mentolado* on its side panels, which translates from Spanish as fresh and minty and was a bit of light hearted fun. Robin is a gentle, eccentric person and a very talented signwriter. He is kept busy in his work by, among other things, people like me who appreciate his traditional skills, and who use them to customise vehicles in a way that relates to their vintage looks. I was soon to revisit him requesting the use of his talents once more.

Some of Robin's signwriting handiwork.

Early in 2024 a Lambretta Li Series 2 caught my eye that was for sale on the LambrettaFinder website. I was not planning on adding another scooter to my garage but there was something about this one's originality, as well as having a reasonable price attached to it, that caught my eye. Soon enough it found itself in my garage sat next to my other scooters, Solid Air and Minty. There is something with scooters that makes me, and many other people, feel the need to personalise them. Whether it is bolting on a multitude of accessories, applying a shiny race themed paint job or, as in this scooter's case, keeping the originality but adding some signwriting to the panels to make it just that little bit different to a similar machine, and more identifiable to both me and others. So, after arranging a time, I visited Robin again with another pair of panels. This time inspiration was to be taken from the song *Jilted John* from the late 1970s. Jilted John the artist was the alter ego of comedian Graham Fellows and tells the sad tale of John being ditched by his girlfriend Julie for another, the cool and trendy Gordon. Whilst it is a novelty song it chimed in with the new wave music of the time with its sharp repetitive guitar strokes and the legendary line "Gordon is a moron", which school kids around the country would sing with abandon. With my surname of Bennett being linked with the contemptuous cry of exasperation "Gordon Bennett!", there was no way I could have Gordon is a Moron! splashed across the sides of my Lambretta. But another line from the song, *Here We Go... 2, 3, 4!* would work. Being easily recognised by others of my generation, it would plant a musical earworm into a person's head on more than one occasion.

Standing with Robin in his living room, surrounded by the ephemera of his trade and his eclectic collection of books, instruments, pictures and memorabilia of his musical influences, I was about to discuss the plan for the panels. Before I could get started though, Robin presented me with the original picture sleeve that I had been missing for so long for my copy of *GIRLGIRLGIRL!* by the Fire Dept. Thinking that was the only surprise in store, Robin then proceeded to tell me a potted history of his Mum riding a Lambretta in the late 1950s, with her friend Arlene. There was also a photo album documenting those long-ago times. Robin promised to ask his Mum if he could show me. I was gobsmacked!

The long sought-after record sleeve.

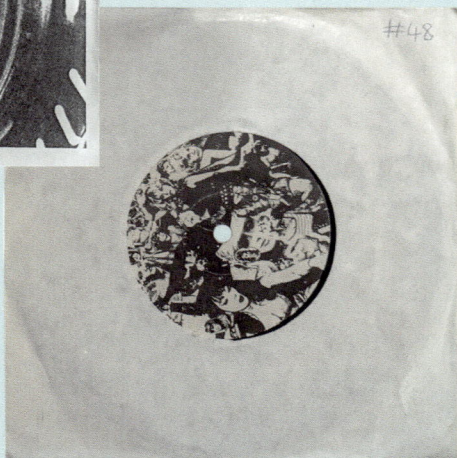

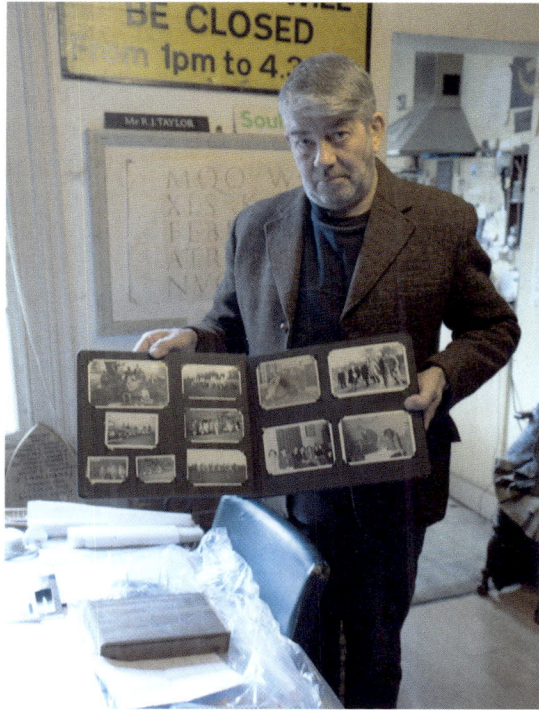

Robin with his Mum's photograph album, full of scooter memories.

A few months later, I was again stood with Robin in his house looking at an album of black and white photographs. The photos were held in place on the thick cardboard pages by small adhesive corners that are now unnecessary due to the rapid onslaught of technology and the virtual albums that now contain our pictorial histories. Turning the pages, I saw old Lambrettas that were new at the time, along with the repeated faces of people and groups of friends enjoying themselves with their scooters. Whether taken locally or on their travels, the pictures showed a time that we all think of as more innocent, slower and simpler. Personally, I think that yes, the period was simpler in some ways but also a lot harder in others. Neither then or now can claim to be completely perfect, just different with contrasting stressors. There are pros and cons for both yesterday and today, but which era you happened to exist in was not due to good judgement on your part, just a chance of birth.

How we used to keep our treasured photographs.

With the photograph album carefully sitting on the seat beside me as I drove home, I was in disbelief of its contents and of the history it contained. The album was part Lambretta, part social and part scootering history, and I had been entrusted with the safe keeping of these monochrome illustrations. I waited to hear whether I would be permitted to share the photos, and the story of the two young ladies who spent their formative years together. Amazingly, these two ladies are still friends over six decades later. They speak together weekly on the phone and would now spend that time together wading through their memory banks, bringing life back to the photographs that were taken so long ago.

Now, in 2025, four decades of connections, insignificant over the years, have finally aligned and allow me to tell the story of these two young ladies, two original scooter girls.

2

MOBILISATION OF THE MASSES

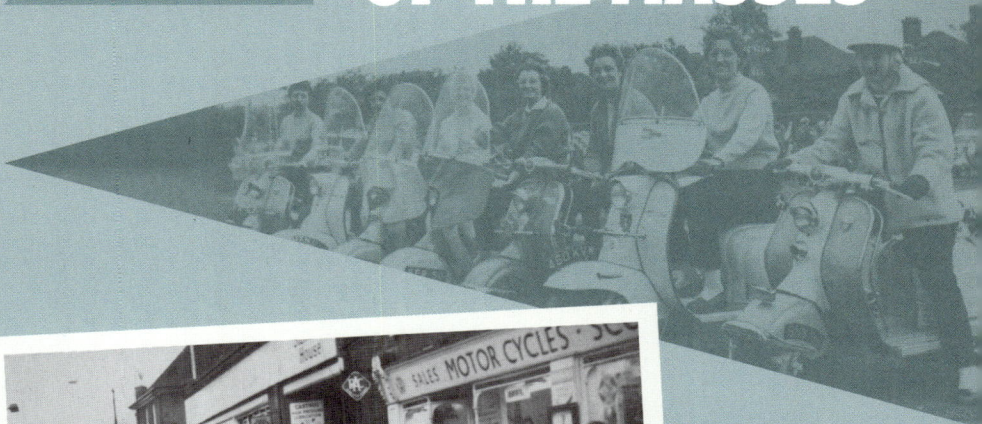

Following the end of World War II in 1945, a feeling of safety and security replaced the fear of air raids, bombings and the uncertainty of what the future held. Over time, survivors returned home to grateful loved ones and the country returned to a level of normality that had not been known for some years. Rationing continued to hold a grip on the UK though, until it finished in 1954, and the British economy was finally beginning to stabilise in the post-war years of the 1950s. Employment and productivity levels were high and the average person, now with more money in their pocket than ever before, found themselves driving consumerism with their newly found buying power. The new breed of teenagers pushed the boundaries with their parents and the rules and regulations that had restricted them during the darker times of the war years. Social freedom was now within reach of many more people. With more disposable income and the spare time available to enjoy themselves, both the older and younger generations wanted the independence that mobility and travel brought them.

In the 1950s, mobilisation of the masses was really taking off. Roads were quiet and sedate, but the golden age of motoring was fast approaching. The ability to transport yourself further than where a bicycle or the local bus service could take you was becoming easier to achieve. Motorised freedom beckoned. According to the RAC, in 1956 only 8 million people in a population of 51 million people held full driving licences. Whereas 50 years later, that amount increased to over 33 million full driving licences held in a population of nearly 61 million people. With an increase of around 25 million drivers over the years, the roads of the 1950s were definitely quieter!

Cars were becoming increasingly easier to obtain too. A Morris Minor could be bought for around £520 in the mid-1950s. If something a little bit more modern was desired a Ford Zephyr could be purchased for the more substantial amount of around £850, and then you could join the 3.5 million other cars on the road at the time. However, these amounts of money, along with the extra required for running costs, were still out of reach for many people. Luckily there were other options. The late 1950s and early 1960s are seen by many as the halcyon days of two wheeled motorised transport. It was the period of the Ton-Up Boys on their high-powered motorcycles chasing the elusive 100mph, along with a huge number of people travelling at more relaxed speeds to work or for pleasure at the weekend. This was also when hire purchase put these machines within easy reach of a potential owner. After paying a 10% deposit the purchaser would make regular payments for the following two to three years until the total amount was paid off, when full ownership would be transferred to them. If the thought of a heavy motorcycle with an exposed engine that could easily smudge grease onto a smart suit or dress was not to your taste, then one of the many motor scooters that were becoming popular may have been more appealing. With their shrouded engines, increased weather protection and sleek looks, these machines often attracted people with the desire for travel and independent mobility, but who were maybe looking for a vehicle just that little bit less intimidating than a motorcycle.

Far cheaper than a car, as well as being easier to store and maintain, there were an array of scooters available to the potential buyer including those made by Triumph, Puch, Zündapp, Dayton and of course the iconic Vespa and Lambretta from Italy. You really could be young and upwardly mobile in the 1950s, slipping through the rush hour traffic to go to work or joining other small wheeled enthusiasts to tour the surrounding counties, or even further afield if you were feeling brave, and the motor scooter gained many advocates that would push these humble machines to their limits and beyond even then.

Of the varied scooters mentioned, it is the Lambretta that is the focus of this story. Since they introduced their first scooter, the Model A in 1947, the Innocenti built Lambretta has long been part of British social life despite being produced for less than 25 years. In the late 1950s a brand new Lambretta LD cost around £150, far cheaper than a car, and ownership was even more easily achieved if bought using hire purchase, or *on tick* as it was commonly known. Because of the almost cult like following that it has enjoyed over the decades, the Italian Lambretta scooter is still highly regarded and sought after all these years later.

A company by the name Lambretta Concessionaires were responsible for importing the first Lambrettas into the UK in 1951. Under the guidance of James and Peter Agg, some clever marketing techniques were employed. They backed their product up with a reputable aftersales service and sales soared by the end of the 1950s, from the slow start they initially experienced. Every single purchaser of a new Lambretta scooter was automatically given membership of the British Lambretta Owners Association (BLOA) between 1955–65. The BLOA provided access to dealer support along with organised rallies and events, encouraging owners to make more of their purchase, and built a family of Lambretta enthusiasts along the way. Owners could take part in regularity trials, sporting events and rallies, close to home if they were lucky or further afield if they felt adventurous. The rallies had an air of a village fete with slow races, obstacle courses or a Concours D'Elegance, where an owner could show off their pride and joy. Rally-goers would wear the everyday clothes of the time, a suit, tie and stout shoes for the gentlemen or for the ladies, a dress matched with a pair of stylish shoes and an elegant coat, depending on the ever changing weather of our green and pleasant land.

Brenda riding, with Arlene as pillion, in a Lambretta egg and spoon race!

This period in scooting history was before the media latched onto the seaside clashes between mods and rockers a few years later, where teenagers were persuaded to pose for fight scenes so that the press could grab the headline news and inflame the public's wrath upon them. The later mods were likely to be seen wearing an old army surplus parka to protect their smart clothes as they rode their machines, while the enthusiasts of the 1950s would often use something like a sturdy duffle coat, which projected a much more genial image to the onlooker. But there were definite comparisons between the different eras. For both, the scooter started off as a cheap but practical form of transport that developed into a source of freedom, whilst providing an object for self-expression that still carries on right up to this day.

Just because a Lambretta has small wheels and a low capacity engine, do not think that riders did not venture far on their machines. All corners of the UK were easily reached with enthusiasm and patience. There are many stories of Lambretta riders from around the world travelling huge distances across foreign countries, either solo or with a small group of friends. And all this before the advent of mobile phones, satellite navigation systems and the worldwide web, while riding along much slower and more rudimentary road systems than we have now.

3

CAMBRIDGE IN THE 1950s

itting on the edge of the Fenlands of East Anglia, the city was a much quieter place than the cosmopolitan centre for science, technology and tourism that it has become. With around 90,000 residents in the mid-1950s, it was not a huge metropolis but a rural town that only gained the title of city in 1951. Even though it was less than 60 miles along the A10 to London, Cambridge was a world away from the capital. With a cattle market running until well into the 1970s, a traditional market held since the middle ages and an 800-year-old world-renowned university, famous for educating world leaders, Nobel Prize winning scientists and communist spies, it was still a part of the simpler times that people hark back to.

There were none of the ubiquitous retail parks that we have today, people shopped with small local independent traders or at old fashioned department stores such as Eaden Lilley, in the days when shopkeepers still shut early one day a week and stayed shut all day on a Sunday. There were a multitude of pubs for people to enjoy and local breweries too, but sadly both are massively depleted now. The main employer of townspeople for some years was PYE. Known around the world for their electronic products such as radios, televisions and record players, they also entered into the record label industry in the 1950s. But Cambridge was very much a town of two parts. One half of the town was the ordinary people who went out to work as soon as they could, or joined one of the armed forces, particularly with the lack of social support and benefits back then. The other half was the *gown*, or the university people. Some gown people would have been Cambridge born and bred, but the majority came from elsewhere around the country. Mostly from families with the ability to support them financially, students enjoyed an education at one of the most historic and prestigious universities in the world, gaining not only a high-class education but the door-opening privilege that went with it.

There were still some small areas of slums that would soon be demolished in a bid for modern redevelopment, but there was no urban sprawl. Local villages were not yet being swallowed up by the seemingly constant spread of building and growth that the area is experiencing some 70 years later. With a low number of vehicles on the roads, railways were a popular means of transport for local people, with many railway stations in outlying villages, places like Stretham, Histon, Bottisham, Harston and Fulbourn, and tickets were relatively cheap, being distanced based. But, as with most areas around the country, the sweeping cuts of the Beeching Reports in the 1960s, were the death knell for many railway lines and stations, but good news for the road haulage companies that would be called upon in the future, to transport goods around on the highways and byways of the UK.

Cambridge in the quiet, old-fashioned days of the 1950s, before the internet and the onslaught of globalisation, was just the place for young people with a bit of financial independence and a zest for life and travel, to scoot around town on one of the new Lambretta scooters that could easily be brought on tick at their local dealership.

Hopefully, reading this book will transport you back in time. Not permanently, as obviously time travel has not been mastered yet, but figuratively. Back to a time in history when summers were hot and long, life was slower less complicated and more polite, where bobbies walked their local beat and kids were scared of the authority that they wielded. Rose-tinted spectacles help here, as while this was partly true, there were plenty of things to take the shine off everyday life. For many people in the UK, houses were difficult to heat over long winters, jobs were low paid, and worker's rights were not always a priority. Food was cheap, but basic and lacking in variety and travel for the average person was limited. The NHS was in its infancy, but many people still suffered and died from medical conditions that are not as critical today. Thankfully both child and maternal mortality has decreased drastically since the 1950s due to advancements in knowledge, practice and the NHS.

But, for now at least, please keep your rose-tinted spectacles firmly in place, and read about the infant years of the Lambretta in the UK. Take a look at a scooter scene that was very different to the one that evolved in the swinging sixties from the bright lights of a colourful and buzzing capital city, and then developed, waxing and waning over the decades that followed, into the multi faceted culture fuelled by music, fashion, the need to socialise and dance, the desire to travel or the craving to tinker, modify, build, customise or restore (delete as appropriate for you) one of the small wheeled motor scooters from that period that we now love to ride and ride.

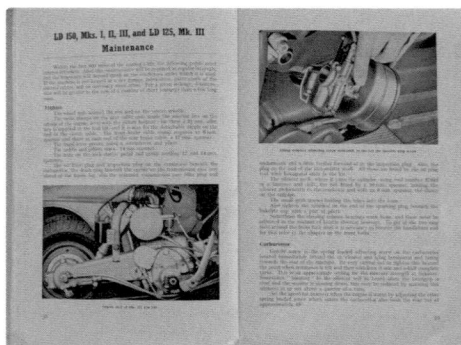

4

TWO YOUNG LADIES

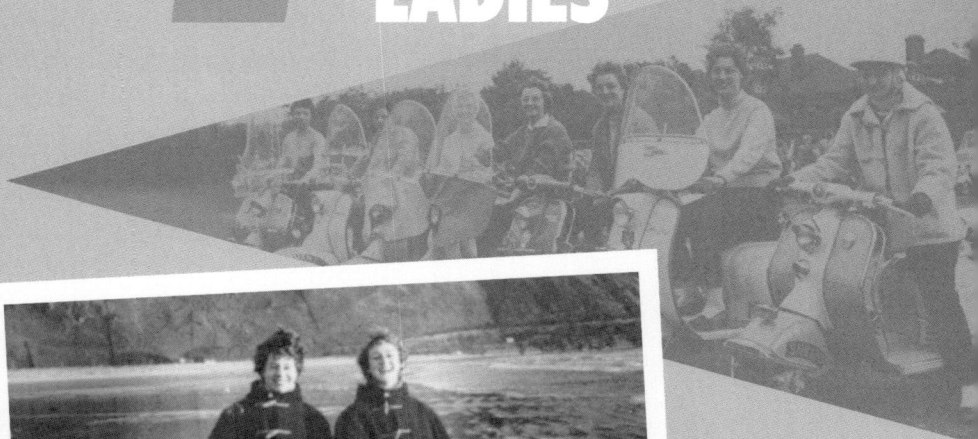

I n 1950, Brenda Bartlett's family moved from Reading in Berkshire to Cambridge, when her father was transferred in his job as an RSPCA inspector, and they took up residence not far from the city centre, in Kimberley Road. Brenda was only 11 years old at the time of the move. She was already settled at a local senior school with friends she knew and grew up with, and did not enjoy the change in circumstances and the new surroundings that were put upon her.

Luckily, the area where she had moved to was quintessential Cambridge. With car ownership much less common then, the road where they lived would have scarcely had a vehicle parked on it back in those days. Crossing the Fort St George footbridge, only a short walk away, took her to Midsummer Common where cows were put out to grass and wander in the summer months. She could watch the university students lowering their long rowing boats into the river, clamber in and then head off downstream to practice for upcoming races against other colleges along the Cam. Once a year, Brenda would marvel at the Midsummer Fair that still takes place on the common, with its Waltzers, bright lights, dodgems, loud music and coconut shies that would be very different to the ancient trading fair that gave the common its name. Across the road was Jesus Green with its tennis courts, wide expanse of grass and outdoor unheated swimming pool, which I can tell you from personal experience, even in the height of summer, can be breathtakingly cold. Brenda remembers her Dad winning some money after betting on a horse in 1953. He came home with a PYE television so that they could watch the Queen's Coronation on the new device, and as often happened around the country on that day, the neighbours all came round to join in and watch the royal occasion on this modern and magical machine. Apparently, the reception on the television was dreadful though, and when the occasional car drove past the house the picture on the screen distorted with interference.

Brenda attended the Cambridgeshire High School for Girls, where also in attendance, was a local girl Arlene Smith. They were not in the same academic year but would later meet through a shared hobby and become lifelong friends. After leaving school a friend of Arlene's owned a Lambretta scooter which caught her eye, and soon after she found herself dipping into her savings to become the proud owner of a Lambretta LD. With £50 from her savings, Arlene put down a deposit on her new machine and then paid off the remaining £100 over the next two years with a hire purchase agreement through the long-established car and motorcycle garage King & Harper. At that time her wage at a local bank was a little over £4.00

Brenda outside her home, on her second Lambretta.

per week, approximately £100 in 2024. After paying the monthly instalments on her scooter, and giving her mother £1.50 for upkeep, she would be left with just a couple of pounds to live on. Not a lot in our modern eyes, but in those pre-decimalisation days a cinema ticket would have only cost about two shillings (approx £2.50 today) and a gallon of petrol around four shillings (approx. £5.00 in 2024), and with a Lambretta LD one gallon could take you quite a distance.

Brenda cannot recall the catalyst to her Lambretta ownership. She does remember saving up enough money to buy an LD125 from a student at Cambridge University though, while she worked as a shorthand typist for a HM Factory Inspector, who Brenda recollects as a most interesting lady that once shared a flat with the famous pioneer aviator Amy Johnson. Sadly, Brenda did not have this scooter long before it suffered a catastrophic failure of the crank's big end and was replaced by a brand new LD150. This scooter was purchased from the same dealer that Arlene bought her scooter from, King & Harper, but who she had yet to meet.

She also has fond memories of riding her scooter out of town and over the gently rising chalk slopes of the Gog Magog Hills to Abington Hall a couple of years later. Working there as a secretary at the British Welding Research Association, she would park her Lambretta under a large tree in the grounds of the grand 18th century hall.

One day at the end of her work, Brenda was the last of the staff to leave and to her surprise was asked by the eminent Director of Research if he could cadge a lift. Startled by the request, Brenda kickstarted her scooter and asked the boss to jump on. Amazed that she was giving such a well-respected person a lift on her humble machine Brenda was a bundle of nerves as she trundled along, until she dropped him off at his home at the end of the hall's long drive.

Arlene, ready to roll!

Brenda's first Lambretta as a learner, 3rd scooter from left.

5

THE BIRTH OF A SCOOTER CLUB

In the 1950s, the BLOA was very keen to boost sales and Lambretta ownership. With the automatic membership that it gave to purchasers of one of their new machines, they sought to build a network of clubs around the country. In 1957, a Cambridge gentleman, David Sparrow, contacted the BLOA asking if there was a local Lambretta club already in existence. A reply was received, sadly there was none at present, but he was encouraged to arrange an initial meeting for interested riders, which the BLOA would support.

At the Old Spring public house in Cambridge on the night of Thursday 27th June in 1957, only a couple of streets from where Brenda lived, a throng of people turned up for the first meeting of what would become the *Cambridge Lambretta Club*. Ideas were discussed, a committee formed, and even at that early stage, plans were made. The local Lambretta main agent, King & Harper, supported the club right from the start, helping members with scooter problems, attending club nights and making their premises available to use as a base for club events.

Club members were a good mix of ordinary town folk, and all had a common interest in the comparatively new Lambretta scooter and wanting to get out on the road with like-minded people. They would explore the countryside close to home and further afield too, often proving that their little Lambretta scooters were very capable of some serious mileage. It was at this initial meeting that Brenda, with her shorthand typist experience, was given the role of club secretary, and Arlene, who worked in a bank, became the club treasurer. But most importantly, this meeting was where Brenda and Arlene finally met and began a lifelong friendship, thanks to the legendary Italian machine the Lambretta.

Arlene and Brenda (standing) at the inaugural meeting of the Cambridge Lambretta Club.

Fred, the King and Harper mechanic, hard at work. Look at those factory workshop tools!

Cambridge Lambretta Club gathered at King and Harper. Brenda and Arlene far left.

The club also dabbled in the new and upcoming sport of go-kart racing, as reported in this local newspaper cutting.

You can't keep the girls out, can you? The first Go-Kart to arrive in Cambridge was immediately appropriated by these two members of the Cambridge Lambretta Club. At the tiller is Brenda Bartlett, the club secretary, and giving her a shove off is the club treasurer, Arlene Smith. Apparently the simplicity of the thing appealed to them. It has two pedals—go and stop—and this model can achieve 40 m.p.'

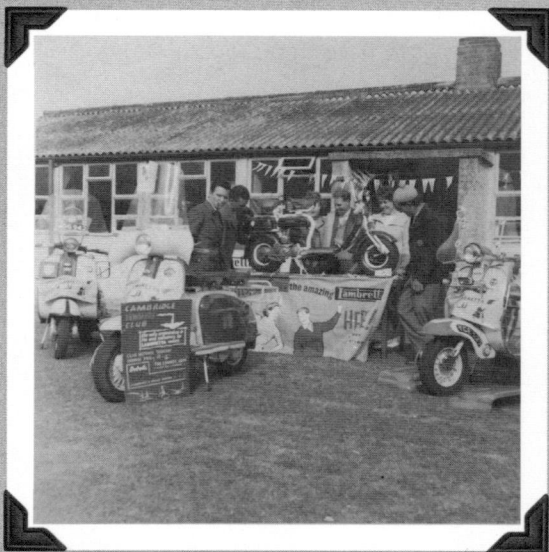

The club's workshop meeting place, sometime around 1961, with an original Rallymaster on the left.

The following Sunday, the 30th of June, the Cambridge Lambretta Club met outside the city's Guildhall in town for the inaugural club run to Ashwell near Royston, the source of the River Cam. About a dozen machines were in attendance. Lambretta LDs were the popular choice, with most sporting large windscreens to protect the rider from the elements. Studying photographs from the day, there were twelve riders and machines. The gentlemen were dressed smartly, as we would expect them to be looking back from the 21st century, with jackets and ties in abundance. A couple of the ladies wore what looked like the popular pedal pusher trousers of the time and a few were more traditional in long flowing skirts paired with a smart lightweight jacket or cardigan. Such a very different time and fashion to now, there did not seem to be a single crash helmet in sight. Whereas today, nearly 70 years later, I would not venture out on my scooter without a complete set of motorcycle protective clothing, boots, gloves and a full face crash helmet, even in the height of summer. Nowadays the scooter scene has much more of a male bias, but looking at the photographs of the day, it was very interesting to note the fairly balanced mix of males and females, and of the twelve riders in attendance, five were female on their own machines. The day looked relaxed, memories and friendships were made, and the weather was kind, so much so that they all decided to make a circular tour of Cambridgeshire before returning home.

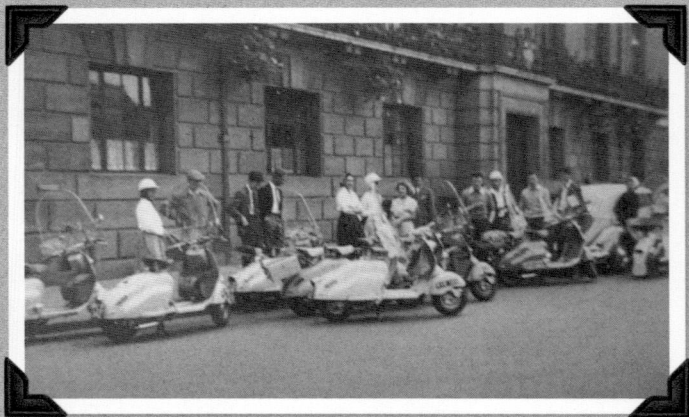

Outside the Guildhall for the start of the first club run to Ashwell.

Club photo, in their Sunday best. Brenda bottom left and Arlene centre in white.

All present and correct at Ashwell.

The newly founded Cambridge Lambretta Club went from strength to strength over the following years, peaking at around 25 scooters and riders plus their pillions. They would regularly organise club runs around the local area at a weekend, as well as venturing further afield too. The first rally that the club attended was in Brighton on the south coast, a fair trip for their small engines and wheels in those pre-motorway days, followed by later rallies at places such as Coventry, Crystal Palace, Woburn Abbey, Kings Lynn and Hunstanton, as well as a club weekend away to Blackpool using somebody's van for transport.

Trophy winners at the Coventry BLOA rally.

NORTHAMPTON
NATIONAL SCOOTER RALLY
1960

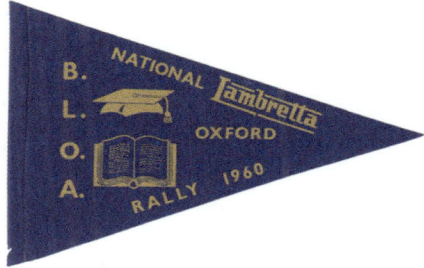

B.
L.
O.
A.
NATIONAL *Lambretta*
OXFORD
RALLY 1960

B
L
O
A
LUTON NATIONAL
1962
LAMBRETTA RALLY

CAMBERLEY
LUCKY SEVEN SCOOTER CLUB
1962
NATIONAL SOUTHERN RALLY

BRACKNELL
'BEACONS' SCOOTER CLUB
1963
NATIONAL SOUTHERN RALLY

SWINDON SCOOTER CLUB
JUNE RALLY 1963

Travelling to Blackpool must have been quite an ordeal, with twelve adults crammed into a Bedford Dormobile for over 200-miles. At Manchester, needing some sustenance, they stopped for fish and chips before continuing on to the northern seaside resort. They arrived there in the early hours of the morning. Packed like sardines in a tin can, they slept in the van until the cafes started serving customers, the amusements opened, and the landlady allowed them to book into their primitive six-to-a-room accommodation.

Destination Blackpool, all squashed into a Bedford Dormobile.

During the winter, when the weather was not conducive to scooter riding, the club would always try to keep members entertained with talks, film presentations on events that had been attended as well as the occasional visit from Lambretta Concessionaires or King & Harper with news on upcoming scooters and accessories, and on one occasion they visited with a TV175 Series One cutaway engine to entice club members with.

Discovering Lambrettas, along with the independence and freedom that they brought, opened up Brenda's life. After the creation of the Cambridge Lambretta Club, she suddenly found herself with many more new friends which she could enjoy the new scooter activities with. They could discover what was waiting out in the world for them together and use their Lambrettas to get themselves further and further out into that new world. Brenda relished the camaraderie that the club brought. They would often meet up for a frothy coffee at the cafe near the Mill Pond in town; where they would watch students and visitors on the river grappling with the long wooden poles used to steer the famous flat-bottomed punts, as they propelled themselves along behind the historic university or out towards the tranquil meadows of the village of Grantchester. Jukeboxes were everywhere too, blasting out the new rock and roll music that was casting its spell over young people. These were the days when the young American upstart Elvis Presley, with his gyrating hips that drove the girls wild, was still seen as a dangerous influence on society and the television cameras would only film the upper half of his body, as below was deemed too sexually explicit. Elvis must have been as scary to society as the Sex Pistols were some twenty years later, if not more. Whenever the choice was hers, Elvis's *All Shook Up* would always be Brenda's pick on the jukebox. One club outing saw members going along to a well known music venue in town, The Regal, to see his British emulator, Cliff Richard. Not quite as sexually explosive as Elvis maybe, but they still struggled to hear his music above the screams of the teenage girls in the audience. Alcohol was not the draw for youngsters that it became for later generations. It was much more about having an easy uncomplicated time which was exciting and full of discovery for everybody involved. Oh, and tiddlywinks! Believe it or not, the club would play tiddlywinks against Cambridge University teams and even had their own mat to play on. Who needs drugs, when there are tiny discs of plastic to competitively flick into a small pot against posh adversaries!

At a club evening, being shown a cutaway engine for the new TV175 Series 1.

A good social life with club mates.

A club outing to Audley End House in Essex.

Riding around as a convoy of scooters on club ride outs gave everybody a feeling of togetherness, and the locals accepted their presence with grace. Nobody was impatient with them and no abuse was hurled in their direction for blocking up the roads or for their slow progress. Back then traffic in general was much slower and as still happens today, they would make quite a sight as they pop-popped along the road. If by misfortune there was a breakdown club members would help each other out as much as possible, with one even volunteering his kitchen table to strip engines down on when needed thanks to a very understanding wife.

Cambridge Lambretta Club
Out and About.

Still a few years before the mods of the 1960s hit the scene, when they would become forever linked with the Italian scooter marques Vespa and Lambretta, the scooter scene that Brenda and Arlene were a part of was not fashion or music driven. Scooterists of that time were there purely because of their beloved scooters and the social and sporting scene that came with it. Occasionally a rider might adopt a piece of ex military clothing for weather protection, maybe even from their own stint of National Service, but there was no specific uniform that had to be worn as a scooter rider. Whatever was available that was practical and functional was called upon to protect them from inclement weather. Many, Brenda and Arlene included, adopted the hard-wearing duffle coat, maybe along with a chunky woollen jumper, a bobble hat for the boys and sometimes a head scarf for the girls, to avoid flattening their hair under a hat if they were just riding around town. On longer rides or group trips, members did tend to wear crash helmets, such as the classic Everoak helmet with it's leather headband to keep it securely in place on the rider's head.

A club trip to Grimes Graves, a prehistoric flint mine in Norfolk.

It did not take long for Brenda and Arlene's friendship to grow once they met at the inaugural meeting of the new club. In their respective roles as part of the committee, they found themselves helping to organise events or put the club's newsletter together. When Brenda's parents moved away from Cambridge, she chose to stay in the city where she worked and where she had built a busy social life. Arlene's parents got on well with her, so much so, that Brenda lodged with the family for a time, and I am sure that their friendship evolved further because of this. Early photographs in the album show them regularly on the same outings, and the more miles they rode together the more their companionship flourished. They were often photographed side by side in a group of club members when out on a trip, even together as bridesmaids at the wedding of Ken and Janet from the Cambridge Lambretta Club, where of course the scooters were on the guest list!

Brenda and Arlene, bridesmaids at a club wedding.

A club Christmas party.

As well as taking on the roles of club secretary and treasurer, Brenda and Arlene helped to put the club's newsletter together. The technology available at the time to print these periodicals was very limited and, compared to what is available now and the quality that can be easily produced, extremely basic. Club members were welcome to submit reports of rallies that were attended or trips that were made, and it was our two young ladies that would create the magazine using stencils and a typewriter, reproducing page after page on the kitchen floor of Arlene's family home using a primitive flatbed printer. These newsletters provided me with valuable information about club events which, combined with memories that both ladies have shared with me, give a flavour of scootering in its infancy.

Also at the club's maiden meeting was a young gentleman that would catch Arlene's eye. Michael Pilgrim owned an electric start LDA 150, which had been named Penelope. Arlene and Michael later become an item, and they would spend many hours together preparing his pride and joy for Concours D'Elegance competitions at rallies. Michael was often successful and awarded many trophies for the hard work at numerous rallies. This was another friendship for Arlene that blossomed. They married in 1962, and both continued as active members of the Lambretta family for some years after.

Michael Pilgrim with Sheila Van Damm, at the Crystal Palace rally.

A photo taken at the Crystal Palace BLOA rally in 1958 shows a very dapper looking Michael, wearing a cravat and beret, talking to a very interesting lady, Sheila Van Damm, as she inspected the immaculate Penelope. Sheila's father was the person that made the Windmill Theatre in London's Soho famous. With its Windmill Girls and non-stop revues, it became known as *The Theatre That Never Closed*. The glamourous but nude ladies on the stage had to remain as still as a statue, for fear of becoming an obscenity if they moved, as dictated by the arcane laws of the time. She also managed the theatre in the early years of the swinging 1960s, and would support many upcoming stars, such as Peter Sellers and Tony Hancock, booking them to perform their act in the shows in between stints by the Windmill Girls. Sheila stumbled into a career of motor racing as part of a publicity stunt for the theatre, that was organised by her father. Driving a Sunbeam Talbot, she raced competitively and successfully for five years in races such as the Monte Carlo Rally, the Alpine Rally and the Mille Miglia. A fearsome competitor, and like Brenda and Arlene, she was part of a world that is traditionally seen as a male domain, but she was determined to earn her place on the grid on merit. On one occasion in Belgium, she outpaced her teammate, the famous Stirling Moss, to set a class record for 2 and 3-litre cars, driving at an average of 120 mph. In her racing career she also astonishingly kept an intact record of finishing every event that she started. An amazing lady, at any period in time.

Arlene, Cambridge Lambretta Club royalty.

Michael Pilgrim with his immaculate LDA, Penelope.

Cambridge Lambretta Club dressed up in all their finery, around 1961–62.

6

EASTER TRIP TO WALES

ambridge Lambretta Club loved to travel on their scooters, and they certainly were not scared of riding a good distance despite the sedate speeds of their machines, including a couple of trips over to the west coast of Wales. Coming out of winter in 1958 preparations were being discussed for the year. Club member Taffy Jones (no prizes for guessing where he came from) offered up a second trip to his home at Arthog, in Merionethshire. Only a small village, it is very close to the Mawdacch Estuary and sits within the Eryri National Park (Snowdonia). Positioned nicely between the Welsh mountains Cadair Idris and Yr Wyddfa (Snowdon), the landscape of Arthog is the stellar opposite to the flat Fenlands of Cambridgeshire. It is surrounded by many places for tourists to visit and has some great roads for a keen Lambretta owner to ride around. A trip over the Easter weekend was duly organised with eight riders keen to take up Taffy's offer.

Early on Good Friday morning, the group arranged to start from outside their regular meeting point, the Guildhall next to the marketplace in Cambridge. Eager to get underway on their 200-mile trip west the group prepared to set off, but one member was having starting issues with his new Lambretta TV175. The desperate rider with the uncooperative machine tried to start his new scooter as the group prepared for the off, but to no avail. His machine's spark plug was well and truly oiled up and stopped his progress dead in its tracks. One or two of his fellow riders questioned whether too many shots of Redex fuel additive had been put into the tank of his new machine on the last fill up. Maybe he also did not have enough spare spark plugs packed, but it was decided that the rest of the group would head off and the TV owner would catch up along the way, after fixing his scooter's problem. When I was a young lad and new to the world of scooters, I recall various *knowledgeable* people extolling the virtues of Redex. I went through a phase of adding it to my petrol tank on filling up, thinking it was going to transform my scooter into some sort of fire-breathing dragon. Funnily enough though this never seemed to happen, and I soon decided to save myself the expense of this modern snake oil. It is actually designed to prevent carbon deposits building up in an engine, reduce emissions and help the engine to run cleaner. Maybe it was more beneficial for scooters back then that had to use the generic mineral two-stroke oils (dispensed from a pump by a garage attendant) that could easily coke up an engine with carbon deposits. Thankfully, modern day synthetic oils run much more cleanly and effectively, and the need to decoke an engine to remove the carbon build up is now a redundant practice.

About 15 miles into the ride the rest of the club waited for a while at Godmanchester, near Huntingdon, to see if the straggler would arrive. With no mobile phones to check on progress, and no sign of the rider and his machine, it was decided to press on further in the hope that he would catch up. Another stop about 50 miles later at Market Harborough followed, but still no TV. After a good breakfast the scooters started up again and headed for the A5, but it was not until the group were nearing Welshpool, around 100 miles later, that a stationary Lambretta and its grinning owner were spotted by the side of the road, ahead of the group! On a mission to make amends, the TV175 had been ridden continually, only stopping the engine to refuel, and so he overtook everybody else while they were enjoying their cooked breakfast. Having rejoined the group, he had no choice but to take up the position of tail-end Charlie with his scooter constantly spewing out a cloud of thick two-stroke smoke and was renamed *Smokey Joe* for the rest of the trip.

Cambridge Lambretta Club in Wales.

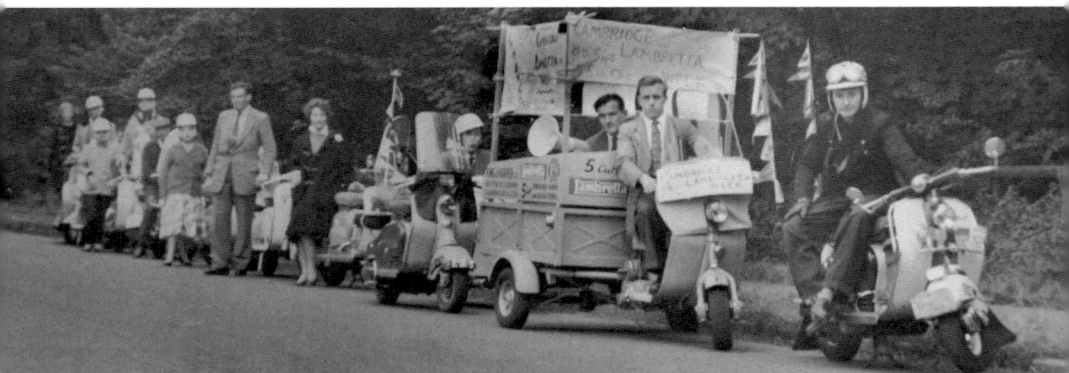

On parade with the Cambridge Lambretta Club.

Over the weekend, Taffy made sure that his Cambridge club mates got a good feel of the Welsh area around his home. Riding in circular routes from Arthog on both Saturday and Sunday, they visited many of the local attractions, such as Harlech and its castle, the narrow-gauge railways at Festiniog and Tal-y-llyn, the waterfalls at Betws-y-Coed, Porthmadog, Tremadog and also walked around the foothills of Cader Idris, before enjoying a tea stop at Fairbourne when they were on the way back to base. On the Saturday night a fish and chip supper eaten out of its newspaper wrapping satisfied their hunger, and which they ate while standing under a nearby railway bridge sheltering from the pervasive Welsh rainfall. A few drinks in a local hostelry rounded off the day and prepared them for the walk back across the Barmouth Bridge. If they fancied revisiting the pub the next day, they would have been out of luck as the sale of alcohol in Wales on a Sunday was banned until over forty years later in 2003. Photos from the weekend show everybody wrapped up warmly to cope with the winds blowing in from the Atlantic, but thankfully this did not stop them enjoying a good tour of the local area under the guidance of Taffy, and they all appreciated a trouble-free ride back to Cambridge on Monday, with Smokey Joe doggedly bringing up the rear!

7

CAMBRIDGE LAMBRETTA RALLY 1958

The planned site for the club's first Lambretta rally was inconveniently withdrawn at very short notice. Luckily, and with only a week to go, a new location was successfully procured at the Cambridge Cattle Market. Hopefully there were not too many organic obstacles left behind by the market trader's four-legged merchandise, that the scooter riders would need to avoid. The new venue was a prime spot in the city, giving easy access to rally-goers and plenty of space for the event and its activities. Having already attended quite a few rallies held by other clubs, organisers would have seen what was required of them and planning the schedule would have taken quite some time. Come the big day, they made an early arrival on site to settle their nerves and to complete last minute preparations. Soon after, and to their delight, various clubs and riders started to turn up on their Lambrettas at the venue gates, looking forward to taking part in the first Cambridge Lambretta Club rally.

To start the event off there was a Concours D'Elegance just for the host club members, where Michael Pilgrim took the honours with his polished to perfection LDA known as Penelope. Later in the day another Concours D'Elegance was open to all-comers and won by a member of the Luton Lambretta Club. Soon after, the sporting element of the rally began with the scooter slow race and the newsletter reported that nearly everybody in attendance took part. Even though this and the following events had a gentle village fete air to them, every competitor would have given their all in a wholehearted attempt to be the last past the finishing post, wobbling, counterbalancing and feathering their scooter's clutch lever as they inched along. The chequered flag for this event was taken by another of their friends from the Luton Lambretta Club, Eddie Johnston. As well as the solo events,

Michael Pilgrim on his LDA Penelope

there were a lot of team events ranging from the mechanical plug change race to the practical tent pegging competition, and onto what I imagine would have been a very entertaining obstacle race involving bursting balloons and threading needles, which the newsletter states involved *many complications*. I cannot help but be curious at the complications, but disappointingly, the details are lost to time.

A *petrol off* race followed where scooters were ridden with only what petrol was left in the carburettor after switching the fuel tap off. The scooter travelling the furthest, before running completely dry and coming to a stop, was the winner. Onlookers were entertained and amused by two sidecar riders having a great time competing against each other. Although both of their machines had their petrol turned off, one had a small leak in the petrol tap that continued to supply the engine with a tiny amount of fuel. With this hidden advantage, the machine was able to cover the course several times, much to the amazement of the spectators and the other competitors. Cine film from the time, taken by club member Michael Gates, showed similar obstacle courses and events at other rallies, such as a pillion rider jumping off their scooter to crawl through a sack, a scooter version of musical chairs and speed drinking of a bottle of milk, along with the more typical balancing and slalom elements of an obstacle race. What is evident again is competitors giving their all while still thoroughly enjoying themselves, in the hope of taking the honours and a trophy home for their club.

Around 150 Lambrettas attended the Cambridge Lambretta Club's rally, and this included one or two other marques; which is often the case on a single make scooter event. The day was closed with the presentation of trophies and prizes by Mr and Mrs Simmonds of King & Harper Ltd and Mr and Mrs Guy from the BLOA, bringing the day's proceedings to a very happy and successful close. The finale of the award ceremony was the choosing of the rally's Lambretta Queen. Many years later in the 1980s, there was the occasional modern version of this event on scooter rallies. Whilst nowhere near as sophisticated, the modern Wet T-Shirt competition needs no explanation and would certainly draw an attentive crowd from the young hormonal males at the rally. Thankfully though, the 1950s were outwardly a more genteel time and the contenders for the title of Lambretta Queen were much more modest and unassuming, with the Lambretta Queen Contest being a reflection of this. Many young ladies lined up in the arena on their scooters for the judging, but to my surprise, the club newsletter reported that the judges were not men but champions for the female cause, Mrs Simmonds and Mrs Guy, who chose Ann, again from the Luton Lambretta Club, to receive the title and Lambretta Queen sash.

More Lambretta Ladies!

Lambretta
recommend
PIRELLI

CRYSTAL PALACE RALLY 1958

*T*o many people, the words Crystal Palace conjure up images of a gigantic building made of glass and iron that was built to house the Great Exhibition of 1851, at Hyde Park in London. Inside this Crystal Palace, countries from around the world showcased their achievements in industrial design and the exhibition was seen as a hugely significant cultural moment in the Victorian period. Once the exhibition closed, what was supposed to be a temporary structure was purchased by a business consortium who then dismantled the whole building, before transporting it to Sydenham Hill in South London where it was rebuilt in its entirety. For more than 80 years, it continued to hold exhibitions, concerts and festivals at its new home, alongside permanent displays of botany and art, until it was tragically engulfed and destroyed by fire in 1936. From this construction that resembled a huge hothouse for growing tropical plants in, a football club that used one of the pitches within its grounds chose to name themselves after the famous glass building. Crystal Palace FC went on to become one of the original founders of the Football Association in 1863, before moving to a more permanent home at Selhurst Park in 1924. What many people do not realise though, is that for many years Crystal Palace was a popular venue for motorsport. Right from the start of the 20th century, races were held on a track of just over a mile long with both gravel and tarmac sections. Shortly after the great fire that destroyed the Palace the track received a new longer layout, was fully re-laid in tarmac, and in 1937 became the venue for the first London Grand Prix. Crowds of 40,000 people were seen at the track and many legendary racers, such as Stirling Moss, Graham Hill and James Hunt, could be seen competing there over the years until the course was finally closed in the 1970s.

Another event, more pertinent to this story, was a Lambretta rally hosted at the track by the BLOA. One Sunday in 1958, members of the Cambridge Lambretta Club rode down to the Crystal Palace rally. About a dozen riders headed for South London, split into two groups depending on how quickly they wanted to reach their destination. The fast party was for those who wanted to arrive in time to enter one or two of the events being held, and the slower party was for those who wanted to take it a bit more leisurely, enjoy the ride and not rush through London as though the devil was after them.

At the rally the club was met by officials who directed them to the parking square just off the main circuit. They had left Cambridge in a slight drizzle but by the time they had reached Crystal Palace the sun was shining, and with the pennants

Brenda with fellow club member June, at the Crystal Palace rally.

adorning the many scooters in attendance waving in the wind it would have been a vibrant and colourful setting for the rally. On site, rally-goers could take advantage of the free samples available from the trade stands, talk to fellow Lambretta owners and have their machines tested, as well as compete in the many events that were held throughout the day. A highlight of the rally for many would have been the mass parade of some 500 to 600 machines riding along part of the racing circuit. I am sure being part of such a large group of scooters at that time would have stayed in everybody's memory for many years to come. With hundreds of mostly shaft driven engines pootling around the track, a fug of two-stroke smoke must have lingered in the atmosphere above South London for quite some time.

Young and carefree, making memories at the seaside.

9

CAMBRIDGE LAMBRETTA CLUB GO WILD IN EAST RUNTON

Some of the club took a short break on the Norfolk coast, at a caravan site sat on the top of some cliffs over looking the North Sea. As can be seen from the photographs, facilities were very simple but that does not seem to have affected their enjoyment.

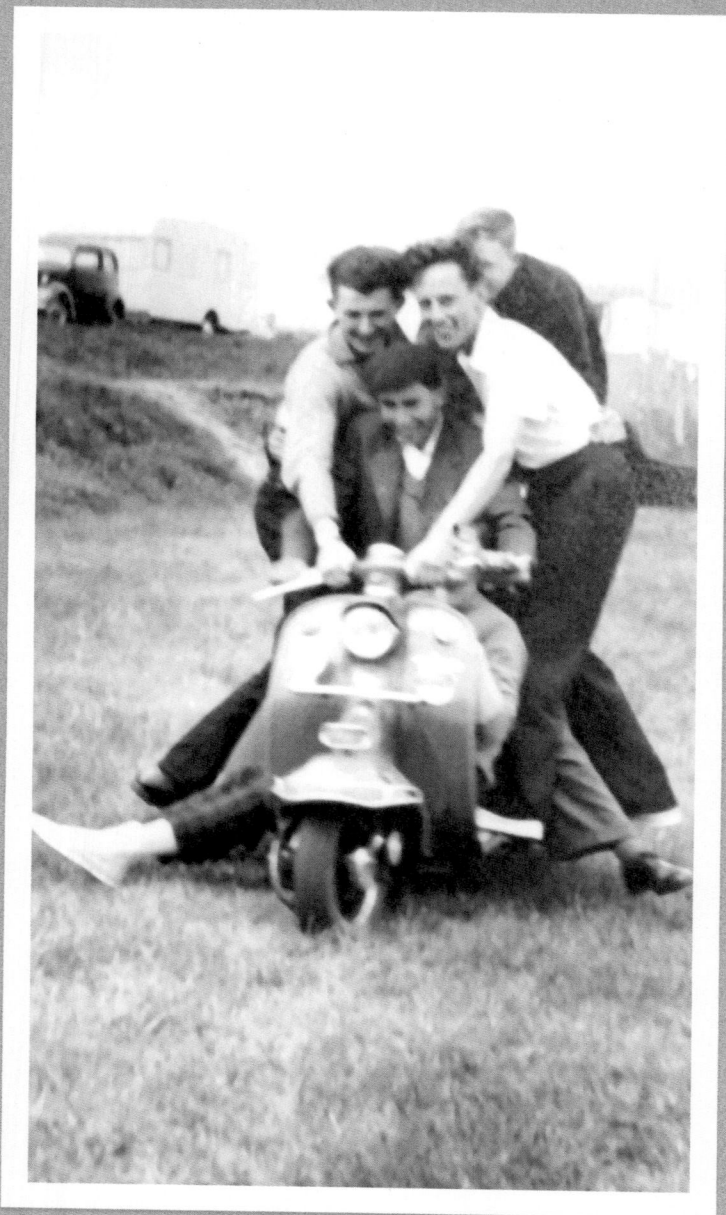

10

FELLOW CLUBS

*T*he Cambridge Lambretta Club were not alone in the scootering world. Friendships were forged with other clubs in the surrounding areas of Bedfordshire and Hertfordshire, with their main ally being Luton Lambretta Club. These local clubs were often invited to Cambridge for guided rides around the local countryside and events such as Christmas parties, where the Luton club once swept the board of prizes in the raffle.

Before the commonplace and cheap hotel chains that are now available to the modern scooterist, visiting club members would often be put up overnight in the homes of the host club, then they would all meet up the following day for a coffee and guided tour of the historic university city. With none of the modern and instant methods of communication available to us today, arrangements to meet up with fellow clubs took a bit of forward planning using the postal service. On one occasion, the Cambridge riders were invited by handwritten letter to visit a club in Bedford for a tour of the surrounding area. Then, in the midst of winter, when the Cambridge scooter riders had retreated to the warmth and comfort of the New Spring public house another letter arrived, this time from the Luton Lambretta Club, enquiring why the Cantabrigians had not been over recently. The letter was enthusiastically received, and a date duly arranged for a visit. A few days before the date snow fell and the trip was about to be cancelled. Luckily the weather abated, and postponement was avoided with the gratifying result that a good number of scooters met at the Guildhall for the ride over to Luton. Brave souls.

After their 40-mile journey, they received a warm and genial reception before being given a tour of the Dunstable Downs, which would have made quite a sight still being covered in snow. Somebody had packed a rounders bat and ball, so a warming game was enjoyed by members of the two clubs. Those not playing went for a walk in nearby woodland to pass the time of day. Then they regrouped for tea and refreshments before the Cambridge club set off on their homeward journey.

Brenda and her family, with overnight guests from Luton Lambretta Club.

11

DEVON AND CORNWALL

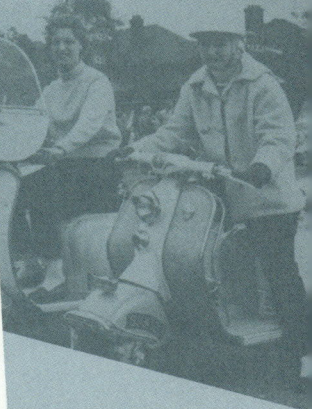

B ack in the late 1950s, when Brenda and Arlene were having a great time travelling around the country with their scooter friends, money was not free flowing from their purses. Club members were all just normal townspeople, with normal jobs and without the disposable income that a lot of people enjoy some sixty-plus years later. I can relate to this. When I was the same age and working for a relatively low wage, I was quite useless at financial management and found it far too easy to spend my money, rather than do the sensible thing and save a few quid for a rainy day. Similarly to the girls and their friends, it did not stop me from going away on my scooter with my friends and having a good time though. Their trips were modest and done on a budget. They regularly camped and used the small ridge tents that were available at the time. These tents were quite cumbersome to carry and pitch, not being made of the lightweight materials available now or with the built-in ground sheets and the user-friendly tent poles with the elastic running through the middle that we now benefit from. They were all still very happy and satisfied with the basic equipment that was available to them though, and they certainly were not held back by it.

A group from the club decided they were in need of a holiday so, after a small amount of preparation, they took off and headed in the direction of Cornwall, on the south-western tip of England. Four scooters set off from Cambridge, loaded up with riders, pillions, camping equipment and all the spare clothes that they could fit in the remaining space. Brenda was joined on her scooter by her friend Jennifer, Terry doubled up with his friend Derek, while Michael and John rode solo on their machines. They headed off for two weeks touring Cornwall, then Devon on the journey homeward. They camped all the while and, amongst other places, visited St Ives, Mevagissey and Bude along the way. Land's End was reached, and photographic evidence was duly obtained at the iconic tourist spot. The photo shows the group standing proud and smiling next to the recently erected signpost, which pointed to Cambridge 339 miles away. Arlene is missing from the photo as she was unable to join them for the first week, but she did catch up with them at St Ives. Her solo trip was a long haul, so she split the journey into two and spent a night at a posh hotel in Bath, Somerset. Parking her little Lambretta LD outside, she unclipped one of the pannier bags from her scooter, walked into the hotel and up to the reception. Overawed by her surroundings and too nervous to sit in the restaurant on her own, she booked herself in and ordered a simple omelette to be sent up to her room before getting a good night's sleep in preparation for the second leg of her ride.

Fully loaded and ready to leave camp.

The weather over the two weeks was not great to start with, and they experienced lots of rain. But, as they rode around the small hedge-lined country roads with steep gradients, tight turns and minimal view, it thankfully improved enough so that they could spend some of their time on the local beaches, soaking up the sun's rays and enjoying themselves. On the return journey they spent a night at a campsite very close to the Cheddar Gorge. I picture them in my mind's eye pootling along on their shaft driven scooters through the twists and turns of the gorge, fully loaded with camping gear and their new memories, in awe of the cliffs and scenery of the surrounding countryside that was a stark contrast to the unending flatlands of the Fens of Cambridgeshire. Arriving home, Arlene remembers having only enough money for half a gallon of petrol left in her pocket after the 900 trouble-free miles that were covered by the group. Looking back on this trip, and others from the time, Brenda is struck by how riding her scooter to distant areas around the country with her friends really opened up a whole new world to them all and left her with memories that she can still draw on and enjoy all these years later.

A long way on a Lambretta in the 1950s!

12

DERBYSHIRE

Probably about a four-hour ride from Cambridge at the time, particularly on Lambretta LDs, seven club members rode the 130-miles to a campsite at Cromford in Derbyshire for a short break. Brenda remembers the site was on a hillside and facilities were very basic; to say the least. They shared the site with a lively Scout group and enjoyed riding both the local roads and into the nearby Peak District, visiting places like Matlock Bath and Dovedale. Simple fun, with friends, on scooters.

Happy campers!

Time for tea, near Dovedale

Friends and Ice Cream!

13

SPORTING EVENTS

ambridge Lambretta Club started off very much as a social club, somewhere to meet with like-minded scooterists, and they soon found themselves taking part in the sporting side of the up-and-coming scooter scene too. Cine film taken by club members at the time shows them taking part in gymkhana events at the rallies that they attended, and it makes sense that the competitive side of people would be brought out there. Whether it was taking part in a road event like a treasure hunt, navigation trial (and winning them in Brenda and Arlene's case) or in off-road riding skill events, people cannot help but feel the desire to pit themselves against others to prove their strength, ability or swiftness. At some rallies, obstacle courses would be more lighthearted though, and test how quickly they could crawl through an old potato sack or how many balloons they could burst with a pointy stick.

With the scene growing more types of events would evolve, maybe adapted from the motorcycle equivalent, and of course they would then attract more participants or spectators. Many of those spectators would watch the riders taking part and think "I want a go at that!", only to then find themselves taking their position on a start line at an event somewhere soon after.

Parts of the cine film show a hill climb that the club attended as spectators. Many of the competitors do not seem to be wearing any specialised protective equipment more than the everyday clothes that they turned up in, maybe sporting a cork lined safety helmet at best, and a lot of them are riding what look like unmodified roadgoing scooters. LDs and Series 1 Lambrettas were the most used models, but the occasional earlier open frame Model C or D was also to be found doing its best to defy gravity and reach the hilltop. A few riders, that maybe had ridden in this type of event before, ditched their usual jacket for a set of overalls or wore a pair of heavy-duty gauntlet gloves to protect their hands. Side panels were occasionally removed to save them from dents while some riders would modify or remove even more bodywork to lighten their machines, in the hope that they would gain that little bit of advantage over their competitors. There were no fences lining the route of the hill climb. Spectators were kept back from the scooters by nothing more than common sense as they rode flat out up the steep slope. If a rider took a tumble five or six people would dash across the dirt track to help them back up and get them on their way with a push. It was very much a growing and homemade sport, and Cambridge Lambretta Club members, having seen the rider's exploits as they sped along the course towards the summit of the climb, would soon have a go themselves.

Many hands make light work.

Spectating at a hill climb.

In May 1963, Arlene took part in and won a regional heat of the *Motorcyclist of the Year* competition, which was run by the Royal Society for the Prevention of Accidents. Arlene pitted herself against 26 other opponents, earning points for her riding ability, knowledge of the Highway Code, maintenance skills and the presentation of her beloved scooter, which she affectionately called Albert. After winning her heat she took part in the final at the Brands Hatch racing circuit later in the year.

Arlene being awarded Area Winner in the Motorcyclist of the Year competition in 1963.

LAMBRETTA CLUB SECRETARY BEAT ALL-COMERS

CAMBRIDGE'S 'MOTOR CYCLIST OF THE YEAR' IS A YOUNG WIFE

A YOUNG married woman has become the Cambridge area's "Motor Cyclist of the Year" and will now compete in the finals of this national competition.

Mrs. Arlene Pilgrim, of 121, Brampton Road, Cambridge, beat some 26 opponents on Sunday in the Cambridge area heat, finishing with only 10 faults.

The competition is organised for the Royal Society for the Prevention of Accidents by the Cambridge Accident Prevention Council and local cycle and scooter clubs.

Road Worthiness

The title of the event is slightly misleading as it is also open to all scooterists and, in fact, Arlene won on her 1956 150 c.c. Lambretta she affectionally calls "Albert."

Points were given for roadworthiness of the machine and for a variety of trials such as figure-of-eights, plank riding, distance judging and an observed road test round the city streets.

There were also questions on maintenance and the Highway Code.

The Secretary and a founder member of the Cambridge Lambretta Club, she has been a keen scooter rider for more than six years and does extremely well in most of the contests she enters.

Useful Prizes

Totting up the prize list at the end of a season makes impressive reading, for apart from the usual range of silverware, some prizes are put to good use by Arlene, who was married a short time ago.

One in particular they valued during the winter months was an electric fire.

Arlene, who works in the executors and trustees department of Lloyds Bank, is also a competent tennis player.

The finals of the competition are at Brands Hatch on July 28.

Mrs. Arlene Pilgrim on her scooter.

the only solo woman rider from Cambridge.

Mr. Michael Pilgrim, of 121 Brampton Road, rode pillion for his wife, Arlene, when they joined other Cambridge entrants in the competition.

City riders in 100-mile RoSPA event

Twenty-five riders from all parts of East Anglia got off to a good start from Midsummer Common, Cambridge, yesterday in the motor cyclist of the year competition.

Their destination at the end of a 100-mile journey was Ragley Hall, Warwickshire, where more than 250 riders converged in the early afternoon. Cambridge was one of 16 starting points.

A total of 47 motor cyclists from East Anglia, including 14 from Cambridge, qualified for the event which was organised by the Royal Society for the Prevention of Accidents.

Three scooters and three motor cycles set off to represent Cambridge in the competition.

There were no prizewinners among the Cambridge competitors.

Local newspaper cuttings of the Motorcyclist of the year competition.

Arlene negotiating an obstacle course, around 1963–64.

Brenda and Arlene at a rally with fellow club members, location unknown.

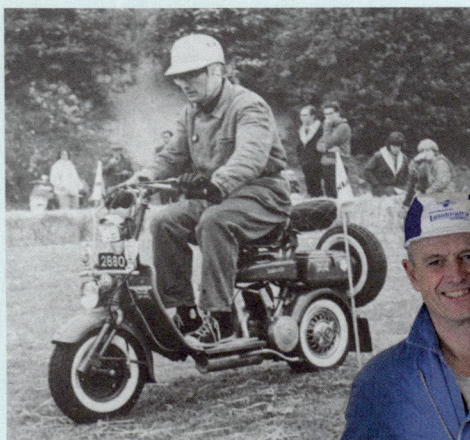

Michael Pilgrim taking part in an event at a rally on his Model C.

Steven Pilgrim proudly wearing his Dad's original overalls, as supplied by Lambretta Concessionaires after Michael attended a mechanic's workshop

14

NIGHT-TIME NAVIGATION TRIAL 1959

athered on the forecourt of the King & Harper shop for the first club event of this type, riders and their pillions eagerly anticipated the evening ahead. Now that spring had arrived the weather was improving and riding events were back on the agenda after a cold winter. All those present pored over maps that had been specially marked and labelled to accompany the attached clue and question sheets. The map and directions would hopefully help each pair to negotiate the local countryside of Cambridgeshire and Essex successfully. To earn points along the way, they had to decipher clues, reach certain points, answer the provided questions and call in at specific checkpoints along the route. The start time of 8.30pm arrived and the first pair set off, followed every three minutes by another until the forecourt was empty, silence fell, and the organisers headed off to their designated checkpoints.

Reading the newsletter report for the event, it appears that one rider had an unnecessary detour to Ware in Hertfordshire that would have cost a lot of time, one pair decided to explore more of Essex than was required and quite a few riders were caught out by the small country roads and some unexpectedly sharp bends along the way. It is easy to imagine these Lambretta riders getting caught out as they rode along the dark rural lanes. A scooter's underpowered headlight beam feebly illuminating the road ahead would give the rider little chance in the darkness to notice a sudden unanticipated change in road direction, and they would be forced to apply as much pressure to the machine's brakes as they dare if they needed to rapidly lose speed. Tyres would squeal as the tarmac suddenly veered off to one side and a stationary roadside hedge bared down on them as the rider hit the panic button. It's a scary moment and one that I would say most riders have experienced; I know I have. As the road runs away from you it takes all your effort not to tense up but to keep your arms loose, shift your bodyweight and steer in the direction needed to keep the scooter upright, hopefully.

A midway checkpoint was crewed by Michael Pilgrim, but he was only visited by three of the nine scooters taking part so most missed out on the hot coffee he had waiting for them and the points they would have earned by checking in. At the finish line, he again sat on his scooter and waited apprehensively. He was expecting the first arrivals to arrive by 11pm but was kept waiting and so wondered if maybe they had got lost, or the set questions were more challenging than he had anticipated. Ten minutes later, the first headlight appears out of the darkness. So that was one machine safely home then. Within 30 minutes almost all the competitors had

arrived safely back and excited chatter between everybody broke the stillness of the night. There were one or two non-arrivals but, with this event taking place way before the advent of the modern mobile phone, a general consensus was taken, and it was felt that those unaccounted for had decided to head back to home, with the aid of the map that had guided them through the evening.

Answer sheets were collected by the organisers to take home, check over and award points to the participants for their efforts. Everybody was on tenterhooks for a day or two to hear the results. And, as in all good fairy tales, who should take the honours but our two protagonists, Arlene as the rider and Brenda as the navigator. Hurrah!

15

A BIT OF LIGHT-HEARTED COMPETITION

There was great rivalry between the Cambridge Lambretta Club and the local Vespa club, but also great friendship, and this was put to the test in a Skilful Driving Competition one day in late November of 1958. These pictures show riders taking part in the event which was held on the old Roman road running south-east of Cambridge. Despite the late time of the year, the weather on the day of the event looks amenable with only a few scarves and hats to be seen and nobody overly wrapped up against the weather. The going looks dry and easy as the Vespas and Lambrettas do battle, if very gently. Sadly, neither Brenda nor Arlene can recall any results from the day, but the competitors all seem to wear looks of concentration as they take part against their rivals or find their way around the course under the watchful eyes of judges and spectators. In Brenda's mind though, regardless of points scored the Lambretta riders were superior, and this shows that the competition between the two camps has been ever-present. The Lambretta riders pictured are still on LD models, and in the Vespa camp there are a few Douglas 92L2s to be seen, with their handlebar mounted headlights, as well as a couple of the latest sporting GS150s. The GS was the catalyst that prompted the Innocenti factory to produce the Lambretta TV175 Series 1 to compete against the sleek modern design and more powerful engine of the Vespa. The new Lambretta was a completely different machine to the LD that most of the Cambridge Lambretta Club rode in both looks and performance. With a completely redesigned engine it would evolve into the Li Series of Lambrettas that were introduced in 1958, but with cheaper components and a more modest design used on the engine.

Under scrutiny, Brenda concentrates hard.

16

SNETTERTON
ALL-NIGHT
RELIABILITY
TRIAL

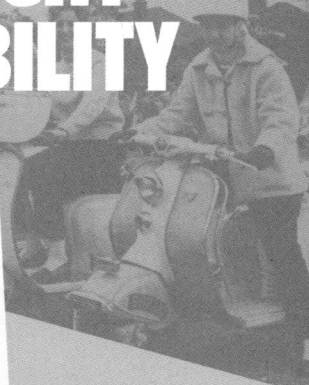

The post-war ex airfield racetrack that was the base for American Flying Fortress bombers in World War II, also hosted the BLOA All-night Reliability Trial at Snetterton in Norfolk in the 1960s. The Cambridge Lambretta Club, along with many other teams from as far apart as Windsor and Leeds, participated in at least three of these events (1962, 1964 and 1965), riding their scooters around the fast 2.7-mile circuit that had been constructed using the airfield's former runways and perimeter road. The track used now would hardly be recognisable to the scooter riders of yesteryear, having been re-engineered to make a more spectator friendly, compact and technical circuit.

Periodicals of the time *Scooter & Three Wheeler* and *Power & Pedal with the Scooter,* wrote of riders setting off at midnight and speeding away from the start line for the 12-hour reliability and endurance trial. After only three bends, the original track took racers onto the 1-mile-long Norwich Straight that ran unflinchingly parallel to the A11 towards the cathedral city in the heart of Norfolk. Teams battled in the darkness, armed with only the weak beam of their scooter's headlight to light up the track ahead of them, whilst foggy conditions contributed to some riders having minor spills or unplanned detours into the no-man's land of disused runways. Riding all the way through the night, and finishing at midday on the Sunday, riders gave their all throughout and reached average lap speeds of up to 43mph. Whilst this may not sound particularly fast nowadays, many of the scooters were probably running the same standard engines that they left the factory with, meaning the riders would really have had to push their machines hard on full throttle as much as possible to reach those speeds. Having taken part in the modern-day equivalent of these events with the British Scooter Endurance Club, I know how tiring these events are in the daytime, let alone overnight. I am sure that after entering just one of these events, teams would have been looking at how they could squeeze more power out of their scooters or how the support crew could work more efficiently to improve reliability and efficiency to increase their chances of earning some silverware for the club's trophy cabinet.

Arlene recalls attending one of the trials to support the club and its riders. She borrowed her Dad's car for the 50-mile trip to the circuit sleeping in it as the race continued through the night, while the two riders took turns to pilot their scooter around the circuit. She also remembers everybody thoroughly enjoying the whole experience despite not bringing any trophies home on that occasion, proving that it really is the taking part and memory making that counts.

Snetterton Endurance Race Meeting.

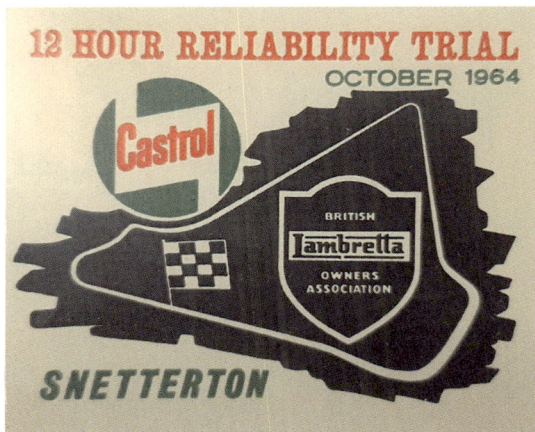

12 HOUR RELIABILITY TRIAL
OCTOBER 1964
Castrol
BRITISH
Lambretta
OWNERS
ASSOCIATION
SNETTERTON

Cambridge Lambretta Club at Snetterton.

The Snetterton 24-hour reliability trial in 1965.

The paddock at the Snetterton circuit.

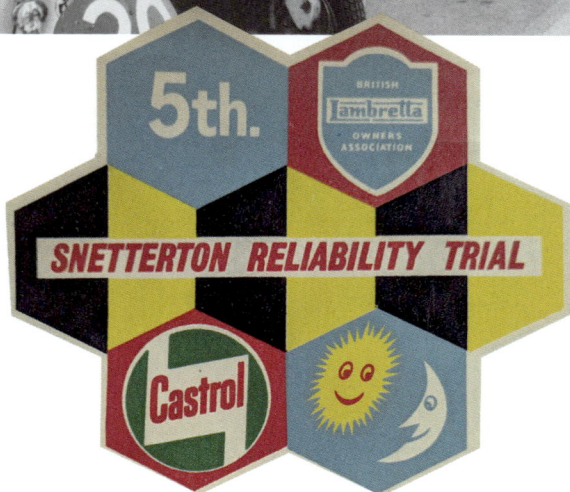

17

DON'T BE FOOLED

For over twenty years I worked in the NHS as an Operating Department Practitioner, primarily working with and supporting the anaesthetist. During this time, I met hundreds of patients from all walks of life. Meeting these people for just a few minutes before they received the anaesthetic for their operation, I would chat with them to distract and relax them at what was often a very stressful time, asking about their life, where they came from or maybe what jobs they had worked in over the years. Some of the stories I heard were amazing to hear. What was profound and noticeable with everybody that I met, if they wanted to share it in that brief moment, was that every single person had a story to tell. I heard some amazing tales and snippets of people's lives that I was privileged to have been told. Whether it was because they were part of a moment in time that made history or whether it was of happy times, an idyllic childhood, hardship, distress, love or heartbreak. They stay in my memory and occasionally pop into my head. But it was often the mismatch between the person that I saw and the story that they told that would catch me out, even if it was not that dramatic a story. For instance, I always had music playing from my iPod in the anaesthetic room and would normally switch it off when the patient arrived. Occasionally I would keep the music playing if the patient was going to have a bit of a wait. One day, a little old lady in her 70s was brought into the room on her bed. She looked not uncommonly nervous so after a quick chat and a handhold to reassure her, I offered to play some music to take her mind off things. There was me thinking that a bit of Frank Sinatra, Ella Fitzgerald or Gerry and the Pacemakers would do the job, but she requested some Led Zeppelin or Thin Lizzy before regaling me with memories of seeing them live at various concerts in the 1970s with her husband. I was both gobsmacked and jealous! This was a delicate little silver-haired lady that probably baked cakes on a Sunday and adored her grandchildren, but who used to see some of the bands that I now revere, and who would have been witnessing rock and roll history when I was but a small child.

And so, I learned to try not to do the one thing that we all do, judge a person because of how they look, before finding out who they actually are. Just because they may not look like they have done anything more exciting than play bowls with friends on a sunny afternoon or dab a bingo card down at the village hall, does not mean that they have not, and this is what this book is about. Brenda and Arlene were riding Lambretta scooters not only long before I was born, but before my parents had even met. They were lucky enough to have been present during the infancy of these little two wheeled machines and to have enjoyed the life enhancing experiences that came as part of the package. When they were both young ladies, they travelled and explored the roads and towns of the UK with their friends. A sense of freedom and adventure carried them along, as they travelled simply without the modern gadgets that can help a scooter rider in the 21st century. Admittedly though, these gadgets do not always work and often frustrate the modern-day scooterist.

What was refreshing for me to see in their photographs, was the encouraging boy to girl ratio in what is generally seen as a male domain today. Engines, scooters, building them and riding them tend to be more male biased, but thankfully not completely. There are plenty of female riders these days that clock up many miles on the road or racetrack or put in the hours in their garage with a set of spanners. Brenda and Arlene, along with many other young ladies of the time, held their own alongside the young scooter riding men and fellow club members. They were not the glamorous young things that sat on the pillion seat of their boyfriend's scooter. They were the glamourous young things that owned and rode their own machines and did the necessary work to keep their scooters roadworthy. They rode, explored, laughed and enjoyed themselves with friends that would stay with them throughout their lives. It is not all rose-tinted spectacles though, and I am sure they also got cold, wet and exasperated with their beloved machines just as we still do now, but they were there, they did it, and they still have the memories and photographs to prove it.

Brenda on her bought from new LD150.

Both ladies are now in their mid-80s and hold memories that they cherish from those halcyon days. I am sure that there is not much around today that they would trade them for. Being a part of the Cambridge Lambretta Club gave them friends, camaraderie, memories and experiences that they would not have had without their scooters or fellow club members. It gave them friends that they would stay in touch with, meet up with, even holiday with, for many years to come. Still to this day Brenda and Arlene share a midweek phone call, and with this book being put together they have had plenty of things to talk about and memories to rekindle, both scratching their heads to provide me with the content to accompany their photographs.

Brenda on a club trip to Southend. Sat next to her is Michael Gates, filming the club outing for posterity.

Brenda and husband-to-be, Tony.

Brenda with their old Austin 7, now owned by Robert Leigh. He drove it all the way down to Seaton in Devon, from Cottenham near Cambridge, for old times' sake.

While part of Cambridge Lambretta Club, they both met and fell in love with people that in years to come, they would want to share a life and start a family with. Brenda met Tony Taylor; he did not share her love of the Lambretta sadly, but while she participated less in club activities, she would carry on using her scooter as her main transport for a time. After a while she was tempted away from two wheels in 1960 and onto four, firstly with Tony's Morris Minor convertible and then a 1928 Austin 7 Chummy that was in need of some attention, that they bought for the grand sum of eight pounds. They restored this car together over the next couple of years, before travelling to the south of France in it for their honeymoon in 1962. Together, Brenda and Tony had two children together, Robin and Matthew. Life can be hard at times, and it sends challenges to everybody at one point or another. Brenda's big challenge came in 1971 when Tony died from an illness, but she pushed on and devoted her time to bringing up her two sons. In the mid-1980s, life changed again when she met Eric Yardley through her work, and they married in 1986. They found themselves moving to Burnham-on-Crouch in Essex, where they enjoyed spending time on their boat that was moored there, before moving to Seaton in Devon in 2013. There they soaked up life on the coast and enjoyed direct views onto the beach and out to sea. Sadly, Brenda found herself alone again when Eric passed away a couple of years later. That did not stop her though, and she still leads a busy and active life.

Arlene still on her LD, affectionately known as Albert, at a rally with Michael on a Series 2 Li, in the early 1960s.

Arlene continued her interest in Lambrettas and shared it with her future husband Michael Pilgrim for many years after. Michael would later acquire a Lambretta Model C, which at one time was the 2nd oldest Lambretta in the country. They owned this scooter for many years, and Michael rode it on one of the famous London to Brighton runs with Arlene following behind on their new machine, one of the legendary GT 200s that they had traded in their two LD 150s against to buy. In the early 1960s BLOA underwent an image makeover and the club's name was changed to the Lambretta Club of Great Britain (LCGB). Arlene and Michael rode with other LCGB members over into Europe at rallies in Ostend and Eindhoven. She remembers these trips as very exciting, even if time was a bit tight for them. After arriving back in the UK on the cross channel ferry early on a Monday morning, they then had to dash straight back to Cambridge on their scooter to clock in and rejoin their work colleagues!

Michael and Arlene on their Model C.

Heading for the London to Brighton vintage run.

Arlene, completely focused on controlling her machine.

Arlene on her GT200, around 1963-64.

Scooter Wedding

Michael and Arlene on their big day.

In 1962, Arlene and Michael married and also had two sons, Steven and Simon. Like many people with small children to raise the scooters were mothballed and activities were put on hold in the late 1960s, restarting again when time allowed. They went on to attend rallies at places such as Torbay in the mid-1970s, at the Lambretta Preservation Society in 1987 and the Euro Lambretta Rally at Kesterfield in the early 1990s. They stayed living in the Cambridge area before moving to Weston-Super-Mare in Somerset in the 1980s. The Model C moved there with them, and they owned it until 1990. Sadly, Michael passed away in 2019, but Arlene still lives there and remembers her scooter days, and the many miles they rode together, with great fondness.

Arlene with her friend and fellow club member Janet.

Michael's Model C and the medal he won at Southend in 1965.

Fully loaded and taking a well-earned break.

Arlene taking a break, with Michael's Model C second left and their GT200 second right.

Michael and Arlene on their scooter at a border crossing with the LCGB. Bob Wilkinson pictured third from right.

DORDRECHT INTERNATIONAL RALLY

RALLY
lambretta club
ROTEM

lambretta club
OOSTENDE

Lambretta
Scotchlite Reflective
G.B. Plate
LAMBRETTA CONCESSIONAIRES LTD · LONDON · SW20

18

FRIENDS IN
SCOOTERING

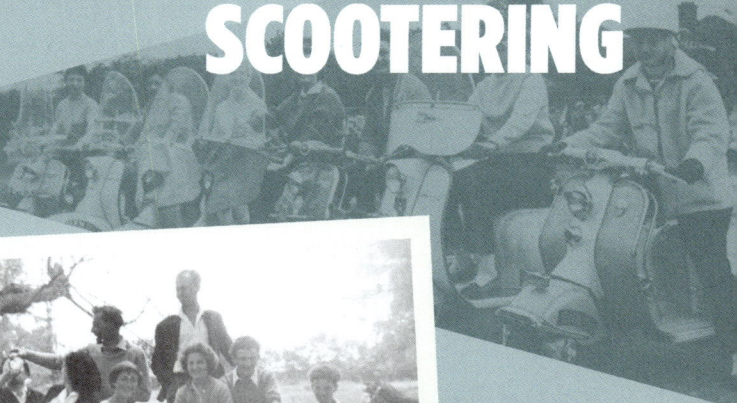

ob Wilkinson, a well-known figure in the Lambretta world in the heady days of the 1960s, was friends with Arlene and Michael and they rode to various events together during that time. Bob really liked their GT200, which he would often commandeer to take for a spin or use to take part in an obstacle course. I was lucky enough to make contact with Bob whilst putting this book together. Now 90 years old, he remembers those days very fondly and shared a couple of memories to include here.

My many years of enthusiasm for Lambretta began when I joined Smee's Advertising as a very junior assistant in their production department, shortly after they were engaged by Lambretta Concessionaires to handle all their promotional activities in the early Fifties. Although I became separated from the world of motor scooters in the early sixties, some of the people working for Lambretta Concessionaires remembered how enthusiastic I had been for the Italian brand in the past. Among these were Peter Baker and Philip Keeler who, when Derek Guy decided to leave his position at the BLOA, told Peter Agg that I would be the ideal man to replace him. I was invited to apply and soon after I was engaged as the new General Secretary. During my time there I decided that we needed to keep up with the Swinging Sixties and retitled the association as the LCGB, which it is still known as today and continues to promote our beloved Lambretta in 2025. My Lambretta years (and there were many) were among the most exciting of my life. I am extremely proud to have been involved in those wonderful days and all the historic events that so many enthusiasts are still interested in today.

Bob Wilkinson ex General Secretary of the BLOA and the LCGB.

A commemorative trophy from the Eindhoven rally in 1964.

Arlene and Bob Wilkinson taking part in the obstacle course on Arlene and Michael's GT200 at a rally in Eindhoven, Netherlands.

Arlene at a rally, receiving an award from Bob Wilkinson.

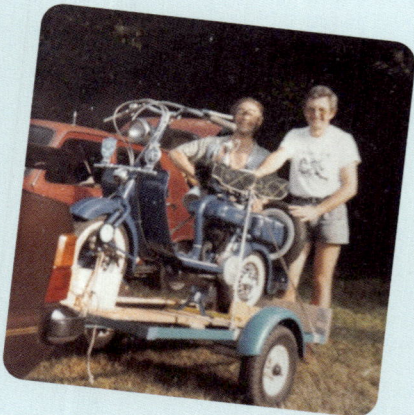

Michael with his Model C on a homemade trailer and Chuck Swonnell (left), around 1984. In the early 1960s, if ever Arlene was pillion with Michael at an event and Chuck was with them, she would cadge a lift with Chuck because his scooter's seat was wider and more comfortable.

1987 saw Arlene and Michael invited by Mike Karslake to join friends from through the years and celebrate the 40th anniversary of the Lambretta, at his farm near Okehampton in Devon. Arlene still has a small plaque handmade by Mike's wife Rachel to commemorate the occasion.

One of Rachel Karslake's handmade mementoes.

Mike Karslake, right, speaking at the Lambretta Preservation Society's 40th anniversary celebrations.

Even later, and at the invitation of Pete and Sheila Meads, scooter friends from way back in the 1950s and 60s, Arlene and Michael attended a reunion of the Luton Lambretta Club held at Pulloxhill in Bedfordshire in June 2005. Pete Meads was another integral link in the chain of Lambretta history in the UK, serving for a time as chairman of the BLOA and as a long-standing member and president of the well-known Luton Lambretta Club.

Pete Meads airborne on a heavily modified Lambretta, scooter scrambling in the early 1960s.

19

YESTERDAY, TODAY AND TOMORROW

Meeting Brenda, Arlene and their families whilst putting this book together has been an absolute privilege. Their memories, photographs and stories have now been given a justified place in scooter history. There will have been many more people in similar situations, travelling the same roads and attending the same rallies. But luckily for us, there were people with the desire and presence of mind to record those moments for posterity with the photographs shown within these pages. Without those people this book would never have happened. Whoever you were, I wish I could have met you but instead I thank you through these pages. Along with chance and serendipity, and a shared love of the Lambretta motor scooter, I have been able to connect with people that enjoyed similar experiences to myself, if decades apart, and marvel at the shared connections. Like my Lambretta Ladies, I have memories and friends that I would not have today without having stumbled into the world of scooters, and I am sure there will be many more trips ridden, new friends met, and memories made in the coming years.

All this just goes to show how much of a hold the Lambretta scooter, and the friendships that people meet through them, can have on a person. And long may it last. However, this is not where the story ends.

20

LONG LOST FRIENDS

Wandering through the numerous videos of vintage scooter rallies available to view on the internet one day, I stumbled across a piece filmed at a Lambretta rally sometime in the late 1950s. The scene was of a gymkhana at one of the many BLOA rallies held at the time, possibly in the grounds of Woburn Abbey in Bedfordshire. On a large expanse of grass set next to a lake, spectators stood behind a rope barrier as they watched the scooter riding competitors negotiate the obstacles of wooden ramps, gutters and see-saws, with marshals helping the riders get back on track, repairing the course or raising an arm to indicate a rider's fault on their round. The film had been given a funky backing track from 1967, *Do You Feel It* by the band Question Mark And The Mysterians and looked to be at a very similar setting to some film I had seen that was taken by a Cambridge Lambretta Club member, and which thankfully Arlene still has a copy of. Watching the film, a scooter passes through the frame whose registration number, SER 428, looked very familiar. My jaw drops as I realise that the person I had just seen was Brenda riding her LD150. I quickly rattled off a message to Brenda along with a link to the film and waited with bated breath for a reply. Brenda was amazed to see a brief glimpse of herself and her scooter in the film, and being able to pass on this piece of film to Brenda filled me with great satisfaction. But there was more to come.

A week or so later, I revisited the film clip and noticed that a comment on the video had been left. Like me, somebody else had spotted a scooter that they recognised from the registration number. Accompanying the words was a photograph of an old Lambretta LD, in its apparently original paint of white with blue side panels, and with the number plate showing SER 428. Amazingly, we had both recognised the same machine. I had stumbled upon Brenda's old scooter, now had a contact for the current owner and also found out that the scooter had only wandered a handful of miles from where its original owner used to live.

Jack Harrison sat proudly on SER 428.

Jack Harrison, in his mid-twenties, is not the typical middle-aged man that makes up the vast majority of the scooter scene today. It was due to the influence of his Dad that he grew to love classic motorised vehicles, including the humble Lambretta. Working as a mechanic he is handy with a set of spanners, a very useful skill when owning a vintage scooter. During a phone call I was able to share the story of Brenda's scooter with him, while he told me how his Dad discovered SER 428 hidden under a pile of junk in the garden of a property where he was working. Luckily, Jack's scooter riding Dad recognised a Lambretta headlight rim through a gap in the heap of discarded items placed on top of it. Eventually, the owner was persuaded to part with the machine, which was sadly missing the original side panels and rear floor runners. Jack took on the role of making it roadworthy again whilst also tracking down some matching original paint panels to replace those that were missing. Jack has done a great job of cleaning and recommissioning SER 428 and rides it around the Cambridge area, just as Brenda used to. One year he even took it to the Isle of Wight scooter rally and rode it around the island. The scooter did not miss a beat.

This book came about due to a series of fortunate connections that really could not have been anticipated. Discovering that Brenda's scooter was still in existence and roadworthy was the pinnacle of these serendipitous connections. There was only one thing for it. So, after much toing and froing between Jack and myself making plans, I collected SER 428 from his workshop, loaded it into my van and headed south to Devon to reunite old friends.

A bright spring day with a fresh breeze coming in from the sea welcomed us as Brenda saw her scooter for the first time in many years. The original paintwork looks slightly different today. Now painted a creamy yellow and a slightly darker blue, it is not the pristine scooter that Brenda knew, but it has had a long life and has a story to tell. The pop-pop of the engine and the smell of two-stroke oil when I started it must have stirred up so many memories. Looking at Brenda sat on her scooter again, I saw a stylish lady wearing a gentle smile as locals admired the Lambretta. She took her rightful place on its seat and, as she held the very same handlebar grips that were so familiar to her all those years before, I could not help but think she was feeling the wind in her face as she rode her Lambretta along a winding country lane, just one more time.

Brenda's old scooter was in a very poor state when it was found.

Reunited after more than 60 years, Brenda
and her old scooter on Seaton beach.

MANY THANKS TO

Brenda Yardley and Arlene Pilgrim, for sharing their memories and treasured photographs.

Robin Taylor, for providing the opportunity to document and share his mother's story.

Matt Taylor, Steve Pilgrim and Simon Pilgrim, for their help putting together this book and sharing their parent's story.

Kerry Bennett, for help with proofreading, along with her continuous support and encouragement.

Nigel Sleightholm for his thoughts, honesty and help with proofreading.

Martin Bird at Bird Creative, for his enthusiasm, ideas and skills in graphic design.

Trevor Peat from Cambridge Lambretta, for the use of old club photos.

Pete Bowden, Matt Stepney and Paul Gillman at Cambridge Lambretta, for their help, support and making Cambridge Lambretta Club memorabilia available to me.

Martin Weeks, for scouring his collection of memorabilia and magazines for photos and articles to include here.

John Branson of Barwell Lambretta Museum, for help with memorabilia.

Tracy Round for her proofreading.

Bob Wilkinson, for kindly sharing some of his memories.

Jack Harrison, for kindly allowing me to reproduce the photos of SER 428 and reuniting Brenda with her old scooter.

Mau Spencer, for kindly and patiently answering my questions about copyright.

Bill Vero, for kindly allowing me to reproduce the Everoak Helmets advert.

Cambridge Lambretta

3 Caxton Road, St Ives

Cambridgeshire, PE27 3LS

01223 516662

www.lambretta.co.uk

From a rivet to a restoration

ABOUT THE AUTHOR

Born in 1968, the teenage Mark Bennett discovered Vespas and Lambrettas through his love of music, in particular The Jam, and the sharply dressed scooter riding mods of the swinging sixties. Traipsing around the country on scooters with friends, he relished the freedom that the scooterboy movement of the 1980s brought him, and which he wrote about in *Taking in the View – Life from a Scooter*. Many years later, both music and scooters are still a fundamental part of his being and have been joined by the new love of writing and creating books. The desire to travel on his scooter continues to be a fulfilling passion and there are plans afoot for forthcoming trips that will keep him busy for some time to come.